Psychology and Health Series:

Volume 6

I WANT TO SLEEP

Why we struggle to sleep – How we can remedy it.

Marios Savva

I dedicate all my books in my Psychology and Health series, to my loving family.

TABLE OF CONTENTS

THE AUTHOR

As an experienced psychologist currently living in Birmingham, England, and a member of the British Psychological Society, I now have the fervent desire to start writing books on psychology for people to read. I have endeavoured to make my books interesting to read and, with a little humour, as some psychology material can get 'heavy' and slightly complicated. I WANT TO SLEEP: *Why we struggle to sleep – How we can remedy it*, is the sixth book in the Psychology and Health series. Readers can contact me on: marios.spurs@hotmail.co.uk.

Other books by the author

Stress

Depression

Know Thyself

Drugs and Addictions

Body Image

INTRODUCTION

Lack of sleep and serious health problems are directly related to each other. People today are exposed to a hectic pace of life, which makes a good sleep a luxury. The benefits of sleep may be taken for granted, but it is responsible for the rejuvenation of our nervous, vascular, skeletal, muscular, immune system, and secretion of important hormones. During sleep, our body's important regulatory systems perform the function of repair, restoration and regeneration. Naturally, lack of sleep will disrupt these functions being performed.

There is a theory that we need at least eight hours of sleep. This is not actually true. Some people can sleep for *less* and still be absolutely fine and normal. With an average of 8 or 9 hours sleep, we tend to awake refreshed and have a better balanced mood.

Sleep helps us to recuperate. It helps with tissue restoration, especially brain tissue. Sleep also plays a role in growth. During sleep, a growth hormone is released. As we grow older, this growth hormone is released less and less, and we gradually spend less time in deep sleep compared to when we were young. During the time we are awake our brain produces a chemical called *adenosine* which is what makes us feel sleepy. By the way, have you ever wondered why coffee helps keep us awake? It is because caffeine blocks adenosine's activity. During sleep, concentrations of adenosine fall. Our brain is <u>active</u> even when we are asleep, repairing itself and reorganizing memories. Sleep nourishes our brain.

As humans it is in our natural make-up to have various body fluctuations during the 24-hour day, which in turn, affect our minds. 'Biological rhythms' are controlled by our internal biological clocks. We experience 24-hour cycles of varying body temperature, hormone function, alertness and mood, and go through various stages of sleep cycles. Our bodies harmonize with this cycle of night and day through a biological clock; this cycle is known as the *circadian rhythm*. Our body temperature rises in the morning, reaches a climax during the day, then dips for a while in the afternoon and finally drops for the final time late at night. If we are awake around 3 a.m. we normally have a sluggish body, we are thus more prone to worry over things, normally exaggerating small events and trivial things, working ourselves up in the process. The opposite happens during noon; we're less concerned about things due to the fact that our body is reaching peak energy levels.

On a yearly cycle, we may experience fluctuations in moods, sleep duration and appetite. In Northern Scandinavian countries parts of the population sometimes become depressed during the long dark nights in winter.

Strong light in the morning aids awakening. Conversely, strong light at night delays sleep. Our biological clocks can be altered by making changes in *when* we sleep. For example, if you go to bed late during the week and sleep a lot in the weekend to 'make up for it', then it is very likely you will find it difficult to sleep on Sunday night, and wake up Monday morning feeling 'down'. Also, if you sleep until midday on a Sunday, you will find it difficult to sleep that night. It is best to discipline ourselves to go to bed at our set time at night, and force ourselves to wake up at our set time in the morning - even if we feel we didn't sleep long enough or well enough.

As humans, we go through a ninety-minute cycle of 5 sleep stages. The first stage is the awake, relaxed stage. This is when you are laying in your bed awake with your eyes closed in a relaxed state. This is where the alpha waves begin, signalled by slow breathing. During this phase, which lasts about five minutes, we sometimes experience various images and sensory experiences such as a sensation of falling, where our bodies sometimes experience a sudden jerk.

The second stage begins when we are in a deep state of relaxation. This is where we are clearly asleep.

The third and fourth stages overlap, and last around thirty minutes. It is the period of deep sleep. Then, after about one hour from originally falling asleep, in the last stage of the sleep cycle, the cycle starts to reverse, going back through stages three and two. Between stages two and three is the REM sleep (rapid eye movement sleep). During this, the heart rate rises, and we start breathing more rapidly. During REM sleep our genitals become aroused. We should note here that our genitals become aroused regardless of dream content.

This ninety-minute sleep cycle repeats itself again and again when we are sleeping. As the night goes on, the deep fourth stage of the sleep cycle becomes briefer, and then stops. The REM sleep becomes longer.

Sleep deprivation may lead to a weakened immune system, difficulties in concentration, fatigue, and carelessness to the point of causing injury to oneself. *Chronic* sleep deprivation can alter metabolic and hormone functioning, which can lead to various biological ailments including hypertension.

You may read in the rest of the chapters what kind of sleep problems one may have, the reasons why, and, what we can do to remedy these problems for a good night's sleep.

Sleep Disorders

A good sleep will keep your heart and blood vessels in good shape. Along with it, it will also improve your immune system, memory, mood, etc. But at the same time, it is also a fact that, sometimes, due to some distraction or work load, your sleep may get disrupted. So, during this period, sleep is not your priority. You often may not be focused on your physical as well as on your mental health, because you are too preoccupied with your work or you're thinking that the distraction is just a temporary phase. Unfortunately, you do not realise that a lack of sleep eventually leads to heart disease, diabetes, infertility, high blood pressure, irregular heartbeat, stroke, weight gain, etc.

According to experts, most of the time, people are not aware of what exactly it is that is disturbing their sleep. In fact, a lot of factors like: caffeine or medicine or alcohol intake, or physical, mental, and financial issues can be the causes of lack of sleep.

The Signs of Lack of Sleep:

You are probably having a lack of sleep, if you manifest one or more of the following symptoms:

- Lack of concentration
- Fatigue
- Mood swings
- Change in appetite
- Drowsiness
- Irritability
- Lapse of memory
- Difficulty in interacting socially
- Blurred vision

Lack of Sleep can affect your physical health, adding undue stress on your heart, hence you are more prone to:

- Heart attack
- Angina
- Stroke
- Heart failure
- Irregular heartbeat
- Clogging of the arteries
- Higher blood pressure

A Lack of sleep can also affect your fertility and the secretion of important hormones, which may result in:

- Irregular menstrual cycle
- Weight gain
- Depression
- High levels of stress
- Low sex drive in men, decrease in testosterone levels/sperm count

We shall examine the serious problem of sleep disorders further in the next chapter.

Sleep Disorders II

Sleep *apnea*, an interruption of breathing during sleep, influences about 12 million individuals in the U.S. More than one billion dollars is spent every year on sleep medication in the United States.

Most sleep disorders can be brought on by one or more of the following:

- Lifestyle changes, for example, marriage, having children, or retirement.

- Upsetting circumstances, for example, the demise of a friend or family member or problems in work or in the home.

- Physical/biological issues; particularly those causing pain or extreme discomfort.

- Psychological causes, for example, stress, depression, prolonged bereavement.

- Substances; alcohol, nicotine, drugs, caffeine, and other stimulants.

- An environment that is not conducive for sleep i.e. constant loud noise, bright light.

Mental and physical problems are usually more exacerbated in retirement age and above. This can cause problems in sleep for the elderly, which is why sleep disorders are one and a half times more common in the elderly than people under the age of 65. Women, particularly those who are post-menopausal, are more inclined to experience the ill effects of sleep deprivation than men. Be that as it may, laboratory studies demonstrate that men are less averse to encounter disturbances in sleep than women.

Some of the symptomatology of sleep disorders are:

- Trouble or inability to nod off.

- waking up too early from sleep.

- Intermittent interruption of slumber.

- Exhaustion or tiredness.

- Tension.

- Feeling disorientated

- *A feeling of being overwhelmed or confused.

Mild medication, used in tandem with a set routine for going to bed and waking up is one of the best remedies. But, two things are important to stress here: Firstly, *force yourself to get up at the set time.* This will give you greater odds to fall asleep quicker at night when you go to bed, and help you gain a deeper more invigorating sleep. Secondly, be very careful about the medication you use to help you fall asleep. Many people start with mild sleeping pills and end up being addicted to them – using them even if they don't really need to. And, due to tolerance, they often move on to stronger ones. Be careful, consult your doctor.

Over-the-counter tranquillizers that contain diphenhydramine, an antihistamine, may be useful for fleeting episodes of sleep deprivation. Since the body can develop a tolerance to antihistamine tranquillizers, they start losing their potency the more you take them. In the event that you encounter frequent episodes of sleep deprivation, you ought to converse with your specialist to check whether physician endorsed prescriptions are required. Benzodiazepines are ordinarily used for sleeping problems, and among the others available, are probably the most popularly used. Short-acting benzodiazepines have milder effects than long-acting benzodiazepines in relation to sluggishness or lethargy the following morning. Benzodiazepines are controlled substances and carry a potential for addiction if used improperly.

Some sleeping pills; for example, the non-benzodiazepines and barbiturates are likewise controlled substances because of the potential for addiction. Although I will remind you, that, as I mentioned above, the benzodiazepines can be just as addictive with improper and unguided use.

Another class of narcotic hypnotics, Rozerem (ramelteon), is a melatonin receptor agonist which copies the body's regular sleep inducing hormone, *melatonin.* This hypnotic is quite novel in light of the fact that it works with the body's regular circadian rhythm to induce rest. These melatonin receptor agonists do not necessarily cause a concern for problems concerning addiction, although one cannot say this with absolute certainty.

Several characteristic remedies have been utilized for a long time to treat sleep deprivation problems. A stand-out amongst the most famous "regular" remedies for sleep deprivation has been melatonin, which can be obtained at most drug stores and well-being nutrition stores. Melatonin is a hormone that is known to be primarily involved in the regulation of drowsiness and alertness. It has been supported, that the ingestion of melatonin before going to bed will help people nod off, although laboratory experiments have yet to consolidate this.

Causes of Sleep Disorders

Rest is fundamentally controlled by two parameters in the mind: one that affects the rest and sleep related component, and one that manages sleep inside a 24-hour cycle. This cycle, which relates to times of light and darkness, is known as the *circadian rhythm* cycle. Scientists support that this cycle is a component controlled by genes that are found in almost all living organisms.

Specialists realize that, as individuals, we experience varying stages in sleep cycles that can be measured by brain wave sensory detectors. This includes a stage in which our eyes move rapidly where it is now known that we are dreaming during this stage. This stage of sleep is consequently known as rapid eye movement (REM) sleep. Sleep problems result from either inward irregularities or outside unsettling influences in relation to these cycles. The feeling of having had enough rest, or a good sleep, is incumbent on whether one has experienced all the cycles of sleep including both dreamless and REM rest. As I mentioned earlier this cycle lasts for approximately 90 minutes and repeats itself again and again during the sleeping process, with each stage lengthening or shortening as we approach the end of sleep.

The continuous investigation of sleep mechanisms encompasses numerous medicinal fields, including neuroscience, heredity, physiology and brain science. A large percentage of the components involved in the sleeping process are the subject of study at the 'National Centre on Sleep Disorders Research'. The focal point is the National Heart, Lung, and Blood Institute – part of the National Institutes of Health (NIH) in Bethesda, Maryland. Studies here include the investigation of the genes that play a part in narcolepsy (a condition characterized by sudden onsets of of profound sleep, which usually last for 5 minutes), how unsettling influences disrupt the body's internal biological clock in relation to the circadian rhythm, and the part of sleep/wake cycles which are involved in heart attacks. We examine the causes of sleep disorders throughout the upcoming chapters.

Sleep Apnea

Unless your partner is disturbing your sleep, you may not think that snoring is something to be concerned about. However, loud snoring can be a major sign of **sleep apnea** (apnea means 'with no breath') which causes your partner's breathing pattern to stop and then start as he or she is sleeping. When you learn how to identify the signs of sleep apnea and be able to differentiate it from normal snoring, you will have taken a major step towards overcoming it and sleeping well during the night.

So, what is sleep apnea? Sleep apnea is a condition which interferes with your breathing pattern when you are sleeping. It can interrupt your breathing by stopping it for 10 to 20 seconds for up to hundreds of times throughout the night. Consequently, you spend most of your time in light sleep as opposed to having a deep sleep, which is what helps you to feel refreshed for the next day.

Light sleep brought about by sleep apnea leads to daytime sleepiness, poor concentration, increased risk of accidents and to slow reflexes. In addition, sleep apnea can result in very serious health problems in the long run, including high blood pressure, heart disease, diabetes, weight gain and stroke.

The are 3 types of sleep apnea:

1. <u>Central Sleep Apnea:</u> It is not the more common type of sleep apnea. It involves your central nervous system, and occurs when your brain fails to signal the muscles which control your breathing.

2. <u>Obstructive Sleep Apnea:</u> This is the most common type of sleep apnea experienced and it occurs when the soft tissues at the back of your throat relax when you are sleeping, thus blocking your airway.

3. Complex sleep apnea: This is a combination of both central sleep apnea and obstructive sleep apnea.

What are the signs and symptoms of sleep apnea?

It is hard to identify the signs and symptoms of sleep apnea on your own because they occur when you are asleep. However, you may ask your bed partner to note your sleeping habits or even record yourself while you are asleep.

Major signs and symptoms:

- One of the major signs of sleep apnea is where a pause occurs during snoring; then you gasp or choke after the pause.

- Another sign is fighting sleepiness during the day while driving or when you are at work.

- Headache in the morning.

- Learning or memory problems.

- Feeling depressed, irritable, or going through personality changes and mood swings.

- Waking up frequently to urinate.

- Sore throat or dry mouth when you wake up.

Signs and symptoms in children:

- Adoption of strange sleeping positions

- Bed-wetting

- Excessive perspiration during the night

- Night terrors (which we examine in detail towards the end of the book).

When should you see a doctor about it?

You should see a medical professional when you experience the following:

- When you snore very loud.

- When you have shortness of breath.

- When your experiences intermittent pauses in your breathing when asleep.

- When you have excessive daytime drowsiness.

How can you prevent sleep apnea? Here are some tips:

Sleeping on your side.

You should avoid sleeping on your back because gravity makes it easier for your soft tissues and tongue to drop back and block your airway.

The tennis ball trick.

Sew a tennis ball inside your pocket so that it can prevent you from rolling onto your back when you are asleep.

Prop your head up.

Elevate you body using a foam wedge from your waist up or your bed's head by about 4 to 6 inches.

Open your nasal passages.

Keep your nasal passages open during the night using a nasal dilator, breathing strips, Neti pot or saline spray.

How do you treat sleep apnea?

If you have a moderate to severe sleep apnea, or you have tried all the self help methods and lifestyle changes strategies with no success, you need to see a doctor. Your symptoms can be evaluated by a sleep specialist. In addition, he or she will help you to get the best and most effective treatment for your specific case.

Complex and central sleep apnea treatments normally include the following:

1. Treatment of the underlying medical condition which is causing the apnea, like neuromuscular or heart disorders.

2. Supplementing your oxygen when you sleep.

3. The use of breathing devices, which also manages obstructive sleep apnea.

Note:

1. Medications are only used for treating the sleepiness associated with sleep apnea and <u>not</u> the sleep apnea itself.

2. Not every person who snores has sleep apnea, and not every person who has sleep apnea snores.

Getting a Good Night's Sleep

The basic principal and secret to getting a good night's sleep is how you prepare for the sleep. Normally, people find themselves awake late in the night and the imagination of falling asleep may appear as an impossible dream. Good sleep may be defined as going to bed and waking up at the right time, consistently, and feeling rested when waking up.

In this chapter, I will point out good sleeping practices along with tips to obtaining a restful sleep. Here are some healthy sleeping practices that are key to obtaining good sleep.

You should avoid caffeine, nicotine, alcohol and any chemical material getting into your body that is known to interfere with sleeping. These stimulant chemicals usually increases your level of alertness and may make you restless while in bed.

Make your bedroom a place that induces sleep. It should be quiet, dark and cool. This can be obtained by decreasing environmental noise and sound; here you can use earplugs and white-noise appliances. Choose to use heavy window curtains or blackout shades in your bedroom.

Some people who have established a pre-sleep routine in bed that is soothing usually fall asleep easily. In this, you can read a novel or any other book that will occupy your mind, though this reading should be light. Take a shower as you go to bed, this causes a rise and fall in temperature which in turn, causes drowsiness. Don't do anything stressful or discuss issues that may affect your emotions just before you go to bed.

Try to do some work during the day, as a result, you will go to bed when you feel tired. If you don't fall asleep in about 20-30 minutes, just get up and do something that makes you relax, for example listening to music, watching television or reading.

1. Don't stay awake for long hours in the night; keeping your eyes in an alert state during the night is one of the major causes of insomnia.

2. Natural light can be used to an advantage for anyone who wants to sleep and wake up in a normal sleep-wake cycle. Don't work till late at night - if you can avoid it, and use morning light to wake you up.

3. If you have to take a nap during the day, you should take it early or avoid it at all cost, especially for those who have problems with night sleep.

4. You should be wary what you eat for supper; some meals are the main sources of sleeplessness. Don't eat too much nor too little as both may cause discomfort during the night. You should also take enough water or any other fluid so as to avoid mid-night interruptions.

5. People who do a lot of physical exercise should do it early this makes their body rest more soundly by the end of the day, leading to a good sleep at night.

6. You should have a sleeping schedule for when to go to bed and waking up, this way, conditioned reflexes are acquired and will help you get a good relaxing sleep during the night.

7. You should know your best sleeping positions. Your body is more inclined to have a good rest this way, and you will fall asleep in the shortest time possible.

Sleeping problems

Most people have problems sleeping. This is normal and usually temporary. It may be caused by many factors. Some of these factors include;

- Stress,

- Sleeping during the day,

- Poor sleeping habits and positions,

- Insufficient sleep preparation,

- Negative and intense thoughts,

- Psychological/Emotional imbalance.

Insomnia is where someone has *persistent* problems in falling or staying asleep. It is a disorder that requires effective treatment for one to finally get a good sleep. It does not require drugs to be remedied, a cognitive-behavioural therapy for insomnia is recommended, known as CTB-1.

This program is structured to help people with this problem to get manage/re-frame their thoughts, and replace those behaviours that worsen their ability to sleep, and they are helped to overcome them. This is very different to sleeping pills, as it helps you get over the underlying problems at fault for your lack of sleep. In this structured therapy, you are taught how to sleep well and learn new habits that lead to a good sleep.

Depending on your condition, sleep therapists may recommend the following;

1. *Stimulus Control Therapy*: This aims at removing those factors that have conditioned your mind not to sleep.

2. Intentionally reducing the duration of sleep for those who lie in bed awake leading to poor sleeping habits.

3. Sleeping hygiene; to change unhealthy lifestyle habits which influence sleep.

4. Improving the sleeping environment.

5. Relaxation training.

6. Remaining passively awake. Many scientists say, if we purposefully don't pursue sleep, sleep will eventually find us.

7. Biofeedback like heart signals and muscle tension. This is done to rule out any biological causes.

Repeated sleeplessness may be an indicator of psychological *or* biological problems. The well-being of your health on the other hand, is indicated by the ability to have consistently good sleep.

How to Sleep Better

It is natural for anyone to have occasional sleepless nights. However, when you have regular nights when sleep evades you, then you have a problem. This could be caused by a variety of things; from the food you eat, to your working environment, biological disorders, depression, anxiety, or stress; or indeed a combination of factors. If you are among those who have a hard time sleeping, then you most likely need help – sooner rather than later.

A research by the National Sleep Research Project, discovered that lack of sleep for more than 18 hours could cause you to have hallucinations, paranoia, memory lapse, lack of concentration or even blurred vision, fatigue. Indeed fatigue is one of the major causes of road accidents. With this in mind, it is important to have a good night's sleep.

Since sleep is always affected by the kind of lifestyle we have, then it is paramount to control the kind of events that may affect you during the day. It is no surprise then, that when you live a healthy life, sleep will gradually come back to your life.

Here are some six simple tips that will help you invite sleep back to your life.

1.) Eat the Right Meals and Exercise.

Exercise and healthy meals are two crucial elements that always work well together. Eating healthy meals helps with better hormonal function, increasing your general well being. On the other hand, exercise ensures correct blood flow while also adding to your lean muscle. Since sleep is a psychological process, the head must be streamlined to allow ease of sleep. Good food and exercise enables blood and nutrients into the brain, promoting good sleep. Similarly, drinking lots of water (about 1. 2 litres a day) is a good way to nourish the brain and maintain general well-being.

This is a solid and crucial initial step in allowing good sleep into your life.

2.) Avoid Stimulants during Bed Time.

Forget the bed time coffee; your brain wants to rest. Many people cherish that one last cup of coffee before they jump in to bed. However, this could be a disaster in your sleep life. According to recent research in the U.S., 50 % of all sleep related disorders are somehow a result of taking stimulants just before going to bed. A stimulant can be anything from caffeine, nicotine, alcohol or any other chemical that may interfere with sleep – including chocolate. Keeping away from this, especially a few hours before you sleep, leaves your brain with no option but to rest.

3.) Create a Routine Bedtime Ritual.

Everyone has something that soothes them and sings them a lullaby. Is it a particular book or a nice song? Make it your bed time ritual. If you are among the few that have not found out their 'sleep- caller' then it is time you found out a way to create one. Creating a routine ritual is conducive to sleep whenever it escapes you. This method works perfectly if your lack of sleep is caused by anxiety and stress; the remedy should be to find a way of expelling the stress and thus inviting sleep.

4.) Your Room; Make it Sleep Friendly.

Is your bedroom environment hindering you from getting sleep? Try turning your room into a dark, cool and quiet environment and sleep will surprisingly come your way. You can do this by having heavy dark curtains, and dim or no light. Similarly, do something to reduce outside noise. Furthermore, a good comfortable mattress and warm sheets are helpful.

5.) Maintain a Regular Sleeping Schedule.

People with a regular sleeping schedule tend to have better sleep than those who sleep at random times. The best way to regulate a sleeping schedule is to do it naturally. The hormone responsible for controlling light - and hence sleep - is known as melatonin. With a regular schedule, your nervous system tends to release more of the hormone in the evening and thus help you sleep. Since melatonin production is enhanced by lack of light, you may expose yourself to more light when you don't want sleep, and to less light as your sleeping hours approach.

6.) Try to Manage Stress and Anxiety.

Stress and anxiety are enemies of sleep. While stress is unavoidable, you can negate the possibility of losing sleep over anything by encouraging yourself that solutions to problems will be found in due course. Training your mind to believe that everything will be okay with time helps you avoid stress and fall sleep. Take slow, deep breaths and put your mind somewhere that gives you peace. Make a conscious attempt to <u>not</u> dwell on problems and concerns that are bothering you, as this helps you relieve stress – you can deal with them tomorrow. Sometimes the things that stress us are not even as crucial as we interpret them. It might be important to objectively evaluate how big the problem is before stressing yourself out of sleep for nothing.

Know When See a Doctor

Sometimes, lack of sleep may be caused by such severe biological and psychological causes that it may not be curable at the home. In this instance, it may be essential to seek a doctor's advice. Maybe some mild tranquillizers may be required to send you to sleep. Although this should be done under your doctor's advice and guidance.

Why Can't I Sleep?

If you have ever lain in bed tossing and turning, trying desperately to get just a little bit of sleep in before the sun starts to rise, you may not have tried one of the many cures for insomnia recommended by doctors, homeopaths or even by your closest friends. Most of the cures that people recommend are actually great temporary stopgaps, but if you really want to improve your sleeping patterns and ensure that you will not have to suffer from insomnia ever again, you will need to dig a little deeper and figure out what exactly is causing your insomnia every night.

Usually, insomnia can be caused by either psychological problems, medication, medical problems or sleeping disorders caused by a physical problem. Each of these problems need to be dealt with in different ways, and if you are hoping to deal with a real medical disease with the help of some lavender and a quiet room, you will sadly come up short. However, if you take the time to really analyse why you can't fall asleep or stay asleep, you will have a much better chance of getting a high quality sleep, not just tonight, but for the rest of your life.

Psychological problems

We know that stress, agony and even despondency can result in some really serious sleeping issues, yet for the longest time, doctors and analysts have been recommending sleeping pills for these illnesses, as opposed to finding the root causes that are bringing about your sleep deprivation consistently. If you do stay awake stressing, or end up using a ridiculous amount of time examining your day, why not utilize the force of your mind to calm your contemplations?

Just this very attempt to acquire the habit to take your mind away from what is stressing you, is very nearly a cure for sleeplessness in itself, despite the fact that it does take some time before it gets incorporated into your every day lifestyle. This is a strategy that includes the demonstration of talking yourself out from stressing excessively over your issues so you can get to sleep more effectively.

So in what manner would we be able to utilize this technique to cure a sleeping disorder?

All you have to do, is faintly envision that you are pressing all your issues into a paper pack and afterwards, you essentially envision hurling them endlessly away into the refuse container, like you are throwing, without end, a bit of utilized pounded paper. Then, quit pondering them until you get up in the morning. Alternatively, if that doesn't work for you, try placing your mind on something, or somewhere, which brings you peace and calm.

There are numerous medications that can cause a sleeping disorder, from antidepressants to corticosteroids. For the individuals who have been endorsed such prescriptions, an outing to the specialist to hunt down an alternative may be the better and healthier way for curing your sleeping disorder. What you must absolutely avoid is to request an alternate sleeping tablet that you mix with an alcoholic beverage, as this will probably cause a set of reactions that can deny you from getting a consistently good sleep, and, affect you negatively elsewhere.

Asthma, reflux and anaphylaxes are all physical conditions that need to be dealt with before you can really get a great night's sleep. By consulting a specialist, you can get the appropriate medication for such physical ailments which will serve to see your sleeping disorder will never again be of a symptom of your restorative issues.

Sleep apnea and Restless Leg Syndrome (RLS) are not as simple to treat. Although we mentioned sleep apnea earlier in this book, we shall look in to it further, as it relates to the other sleep problems.

Changes in Habits

a) Distance yourself from alcohol, smoking and sleeping pills.

b) On the off chance that you have exorbitant weight, you need to diminish it. Indeed, a small loss of weight can help you in your quest for curing sleep apnea.

c) Sleep on your side rather than your back. Sleeping on your side can help to keep your throat open. Individuals with either moderate or genuine apnea of sleep will need to make this change.

Ceaseless Positive Airway Pressure (CPAP)

CPAP is the basic system widely used to cure sleep apnea in individuals. For this, you have a veil draped over your nose throughout the your sleep. The veil allows the air in your throat to enter with a mild air pressure which is specific for you. The expanded weight of air as you breathe allows the throat to stay open while you sleep. The air pressure is thus balanced according to your breathing. CPAP machines are now commonly used for this process.

Surgery

Some individuals with sleep apnea may profit from surgery. The kind of surgery depends on upon the reason for the sleep apnea. Surgery may be carried out to uproot the tonsils and adenoids if they are the culprits for the sleep apnea, since they are obstructing the respiratory route.

Medicinal Therapy

There is no medication for the cure of Obstructive Sleep Apnea (OSA). Oral administration of methylxanthine or theophylline although may help a little as a cure for sleep apnea, can additionally generate other counter-productive symptoms, for example, palpitations and sleep deprivation. Theophylline is by and large insufficient in older people with OSA, however it is frequently used to cure <u>Central</u> Sleep Apnea.

Bi-level Positive Airway Pressure

Another alternative for the cure for sleep apnea is otherwise known as Bi-level Positive Airway Pressure (BPAP) which utilizes an electronic circuit to regulate the patient's breathing, and gives two separate air pressures, a higher one during inhaling and an lower one during exhalation. It uses a continuous positive airway pressure system with a time-cycled or flow-cycled change during functioning.

Sleeping Pills

One of the biggest health threats created by our busy modern lifestyles is a lack of sleep. Whether due to stress, working long hours or simply watching too much TV - more and more of us are starting to suffer from a serious lack of sleep, which can then wreak havoc with a person's overall mental and physical health.

While too little sleep can cause plenty of health issues on its own, there may even be a potentially more serious problem caused by how we deal with these issues – namely, that a huge percentage of us choose to deal with our lack of rest by popping sleeping pills. No matter whether they're prescription or you obtained them over the counter, there is an overwhelming amount of evidence that points to the negative long term use of sleeping pills. I can't stress this enough.

Far from helping to cure your problems, sleeping pills simply serve to *mask* the problem instead of seeking to diagnose and treat the underlying causes. This in turn, usually only prolongs and exacerbates the sleeping problems and often even makes them worse. Still more worrying, is the fact that long term use of many of the most common sleeping medications themselves have also been shown to contribute to a number of other physical and mental disorders.

Short Term vs Long Term Effectiveness

There's no doubt that all of us suffer from sleeping problems at one time or another, and that most of us have simply grown used to it as a fact of life. Luckily though, for most of us, these problems are usually temporary, but that still doesn't make it less of a problem when you can't sleep the night before that long day at work, or looking after young infants or children.

It is situations just like these that sleeping medications are made for, as they have been shown to be incredibly effective in dealing

35

with short term sleeping problems caused by stress, travel, etc. However, the problem comes when people attempt to treat more serious sleeping disorders like insomnia with sleeping medications due to the negative long term effects of using sleeping pills.

Sleep and Mental Health

While taking a sleeping pill may help you get the rest you need before that big meeting, continually struggling to get a full night's rest for long periods is usually the sign of a potentially more serious underlying issue. The biggest problem with long term use of sleeping medications is that they don't take this underlying cause into account, which is bad enough, but even worse when you consider that a huge majority of sleeping problems are caused by depression or other mental health disorders.

When left untreated, depression almost always worsens, which shows just how dangerous ignoring the underlying causes of insomnia can be. According to sleep specialists at Harvard Medical School, although sleeping problems were once thought of as merely a symptom of depression and other psychological disorders, research now shows that in many cases the sleeping problems often make the mental issues much worse.

Sleeping Pills and Dependency

While one issue is sleeping pills not treating the underlying causes of the problem, another issue altogether is the link between sleeping medications and mental or physical dependency.

Although there has been a large rise in the use of supposedly non-habit forming, over-the-counter sleeping medications in recent years, many people with more serious sleeping disorders continue to rely on sedative or hypnotic sleeping pills, the vast majority of which, have been shown to be quite addictive when used for longer periods.

By far the most commonly prescribed group of sedative-hypnotic sleeping medications is benzodiazepines, which also act as anti-anxiety medications. Among this group are the popular drugs Xanax and Valium, both of which can be very addictive, even if only taken for a week or two.

The problem with drugs like these doesn't lie in their role in helping make a person drowsy and more able to fall asleep, but rather the way they make a person feel mentally. Ask anyone who's taken these medications and they'll probably tell you that they instantly make them feel happy and confident, which may be a good thing in the short term, but can cause them to become mentally addicted to the drug, and only feel happy when they're taking it. Typically, the rest of time they are downcast.

Due to their potentially habit-forming nature, both the American Psychological Association and the American Academy of Sleep Medicine recommend that people exhibiting signs of any long term sleeping issues should completely avoid the use of these, or any other sleeping medications, and instead seek out alternative forms of treatment such as Cognitive Behavioural Therapy (CBT) or progressive relaxation therapy.

The Psychology Behind Sleep

Medical research has shown that sleep is one of the most important factors contributing to our overall level of health and well-being. However, if you were to survey a group of doctors, they would likely, almost unanimously agree, that sleep is the one area of health that we ignore more than the others. More and more people are starting to concern themselves with eating a healthy, balanced diet and leading an active lifestyle, yet an overwhelming majority of us continue to go through life tired and worn down due to not getting enough sleep.

The simple fact is that getting around eight full hours of restful sleep each night will do as much to keep a person healthy as proper diet and exercise, yet most of us are continuing to let our sleep deficits build up due to our modern, hectic lifestyles. Still, it's never too late to begin focusing on your sleep patterns to ensure your body and mind get the rest they so desperately need, and by doing so, you may be able to not only prolong your life, but also hopefully ensure your last years are as good as your first ones.

The Role of Sleep in Mental Health

One of the biggest problems facing our society is the fact that we're continuing to try to live on less and less sleep. In all but the most recent past, our lives were basically dictated by the sun, as people would wake up when the sun came up and settle down for the evening as the sun set—mostly due to a lack of light.

However, with the advent of electricity, humans were suddenly able to stay awake and active long after the sun went down, which definitely allowed for greater productivity and largely contributed to building our modern, technologically advanced world. In fact, there's no doubt that sleeping fewer hours has been a major factor in human advancement. However, the one problem with all of this, is that a lack of sleep can and will adversely affect not only our physical health and well-being, but also our mental state.

The Link Between Lack of Sleep and Depression

Lots of research has been done to determine the extent of the link between sleep (or a lack of) and depression, as there is no doubt that the two are inextricably connected in one way or another. It has long been known that insomnia and other sleeping disorders are quite common amongst depressed people, but it wasn't until recently that we started to better understand just how deep the connection between sleep and mental health really is.

According to the National Sleep Foundation, the relationship between sleeping disorders and depression is so intertwined that each condition is often either the cause, or result of, the other. In fact, individuals suffering from insomnia are ten times more likely to become depressed than those with normal sleeping patterns, showing just how important restful sleep is to your overall health.

Curing Sleeping Problems with the Help of Psychology

As the field of psychology has begun to allow us to further understand the deep connection that exists between sleep and mental health, it only stands to reason that it may also be able to play a role in helping us develop better cures for society's growing sleep problems. Currently, much research is being done in the field of cognitive behavioural therapy (CBT) and its usefulness in treating insomnia and other sleeping disorders.

CBT has been shown to be so effective, that it is now the treatment of choice for most sleep specialists. Even as far back as 2001, a study in the Journal of the American Medicinal Association found CBT to be the most effective of all of the various insomnia treatments tested.

CBT seeks to treat insomnia and other sleeping disorders by taking a two-fold approach and dealing with both the mental and physical causes of sleeping problems. First, the cognitive or mental approach, focuses on erasing the common misconceptions and unrealistic expectations associated with sleep that people with insomnia often dwell on, such as that we *always* need 8 hours sleep or, continuing to look at the clock and count how many hours until we have to get up.

During the treatment, a psychologist will work with the patient to develop more realistic expectations and ideas about their sleeping patterns, while at the same time working to change their behavioural patterns in a way that's more conducive to deep, restful sleep, such as making sure to eliminate artificial lighting and turning off electronic devices at least an hour before going to bed.

Not everyone has the same sleep needs; some people are fine with only three or four hours while others need ten hours a night or more. Still, at the end of the day, it's impossible to ignore the link between sleep and mental/physical health, showing just how important it is that we start to take our society's growing sleep problems more seriously.

Night Terrors

Some children, and to a lesser extent, adults, can experience what is known as *night terrors*. An individual suffering from this type of sleep disorder will typically sit up after awaking from sleep in a state of high arousal and with the appearance of being terrified, and might start walking around, speaking incoherently. The accompanying bodily symptoms are a dramatic increase in heart rate and breathing rate. A person who suffers from night terror rarely wakes up completely *during* the episode. The next morning the individual will typically remember very little, if anything at all. Sometimes, a fleeting image will be recollected, mainly a frightening one. Night terrors are not the same as, or classed as, nightmares. Both dreams and nightmares occur during REM sleep, early in the morning.

Night terrors occur the during the first few hours of the 4th stage in the sleep cycle. The person who suffers from this kind of sleep disorder is usually woken up by a member of the family when going through a night terror episode.

Sleepwalking also occurs during the first hours of stage 4 in the sleep cycle. Scientists who have researched this area have found that sleepwalking, as well as sleep talking, is hereditary. Those individuals who sleepwalk do not have a recollection of having done so, and it is usually harmless when it happens.

Night terrors occur more often in children, the same applies for sleepwalking. Children have a deeper and longer stage 4 sleep than adults. This 4th stage in the 90 minute sleep cycle shortens as we grow older, consequently, so does the sleepwalking and night terrors.

When we dream, we sometimes experience a fleeting awareness that we are in fact dreaming. These type of dreams are what we call <u>lucid</u> dreams. When we dream, which occurs in REM sleep, we more often than not, experience negative emotions. We also mostly have dreams related to our everyday lives. What is important though to remember, is that we absolutely need REM sleep. And the dreaming part that goes with it.

A Little Knowledge can Go a Long Way

Some people worry unnecessarily about their sleep. Although people who suffer from insomnia *do* get less sleep than others, they usually overestimate how long it took them to fall asleep. They also tend to *underestimate* how long they actually sleep. If you have been awake for an hour or so, you will tend to think you've only had very little sleep. This is because it is normally the waking part you remember.

For remedying full-blown insomnia, those people who use sleeping pills or alcohol can worsen the problem. These reduce REM sleep and tend to leave someone feeling 'down' the next day. A tolerance of the body develops, meaning larger doses and amounts required to achieve the same effect. If consumption of pills or alcohol is stopped, the insomnia will likely worsen. Research is being carried out on substances that already exist and abound during sleep, with the aim of synthesizing them as an aid for sleep, but without the negative side effects.

We have mentioned earlier some measures which we can take to help us sleep. We shall mention a few more that I believe are the most important, some of which I have already touched upon:

- Avoid caffeine intake after around 5 or 6 pm. Also, avoid rich foods and chocolate before bedtime.

- Try and exercise often, but not late in the evening.

- Try a glass of milk! Milk contains those substances which manufacture serotonin, a neurotransmitter in the brain which facilitates sleep.

- Have a relaxing/calming down routine that you can do before you go to bed.

- Dim lighting is conducive in aiding drowsiness that leads to sleep.

- Know (and keep reminding yourself) that <u>temporary</u> loss of sleep doesn't cause any great harm, so, don't stress about it.

- Keep to a regular sleeping schedule; get up from bed the same time everyday - even after a bad night's sleep, and even after no night's sleep at all.

- Pray. If you are an individual who likes to pray, it has been well documented that prayer before laying in bed quietens the mind, lessens the intensity of our thoughts, releases tension in the body and calms the spirit.

- If you feel that nothing you do is helping you, then it is a good idea – as a last resort – to purposely get less sleep. Either get up earlier than you normally would, or, go to bed later than you normally do.

The above simple steps can make a big difference. If you are not able to do most, or some of them, try at least to perform one of them. That simple step you may take, may make a big difference to you.

 # Afterword

As we have mentioned in the beginning of this book, a lack of sleep and serious health problems are directly related to each other. Today, we are exposed to such a hectic pace of life, it makes a good sleep a luxury. The benefits of sleep can be taken for granted, but it is responsible for the rejuvenation of our nervous, vascular, skeletal, muscular, immune system, and secretion of important hormones. During sleep, our body's important regulatory systems perform the function of repair, restoration and regeneration. Naturally, lack of sleep will disrupt these functions being performed.

Unfortunately, we noted that more and more people are starting to concern themselves with eating a healthy, balanced diet and leading an active lifestyle, and yet an overwhelming majority of us continue to go through life tired and worn down due to not getting enough sleep. Getting around eight full hours of restful sleep each night will do as much to keep a person healthy as proper diet and exercise, yet most of us are continuing to let our sleep deficits build up due to our modern, hectic lifestyles.

It's never too late though to begin focusing on your sleep patterns to ensure your body and mind get the rest they so desperately need, and by doing so, you may be able to not only prolong your life, but also hopefully ensure your last years are as good as your first ones.

Remember, since sleep is always affected by the kind of lifestyle we have, then it is paramount to control the kind of events that may affect you during the day. It is no surprise then, that when you make positive changes to your lifestyle, sleep will gradually come back to your life.

I hope you enjoyed this book.

The Psychology and Health series

Stress: We Can Master It.

Depression and Sadness: Never Lose Hope – Even If You Can't See Any.

Drugs and Addictions: Some Things You Might Know, A lot of Things You Might Not.

Body Image: How We See Ourselves and Others; How This Can Lead to Problems.

Know Thyself: The Eternal Struggle of The Heart and Mind.

I Want to Sleep: Why We Struggle to Sleep – How We Can Remedy It.

www.ingramcontent.com/pod-product-compliance
Lightning Source LLC
Chambersburg PA
CBHW070233290526
45789CB00004B/1599